Meet the Morgans

The Stars of the
Morgan Horse Series

Willow Bend Publishing
Goshen, Massachusetts

We gratefully acknowledge the permission of the following photographers to use their photos in Meet the Morgans:

Bob Moseder, Flagler Beach, FL
©Stan Phaneuf, Newbury, VT
Lorna Drake, Freudy Photos Archives, LLC
Breyer Animal Creations, photos taken by Jennifer Munson
Debbie Uecker-Keough, El Cajon, CA
Krista Allenby, Give A Hoot Vintage, Northampton, MA
Holly Rebecca Feld, Goshen, MA

Cover and text design by Jennifer Conlan

Library of Congress Control Number: 2012935620
ISBN: 978-0-9831138-4-3

Direct inquiries to:
Willow Bend Publishing
P.O. Box 304
Goshen, MA 01032
413-268-3461
www.willowbendpublishing.com

Printed in Korea

10 9 8 7 6 5 4 3 2

Dedication

To every child who has ever dreamed of owning a horse.
Dreams do come true!

Author's Note

While the books of the Morgan Horse series are works of fiction, I have based all the main equine characters on my own horses. Beyond the simple physical attributes, I have used each animal's unique behaviors, quirks, and traits to create characters who are realistic. Frequently, when readers learn that the horses I write about are based on ones I own, they ask me to share photographs of their favorites. After several years of hearing this request, I decided to oblige my fans, and *Meet the Morgans* was born. I hope you enjoy meeting my beloved best friends as much as I've enjoyed putting this tribute to them together.

— Ellen F. Feld

Blackjack

Rum Brook Immortal Star*
(Immortal Command x Rum Brook Aphrodite)

*This is Blackjack's registered name, recorded with The American Morgan Horse Association. The names in parentheses are Blackjack's parents, with his father listed first.

Bob Moseder

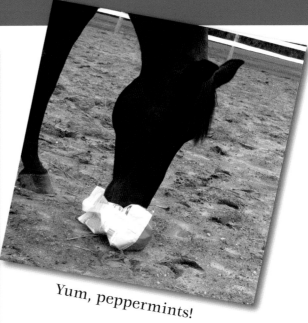

Yum, peppermints!

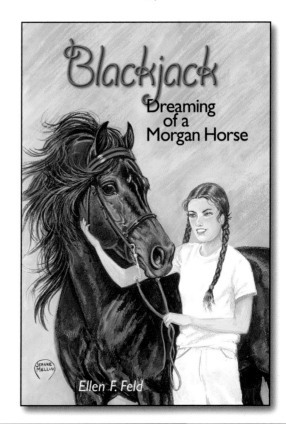

Blackjack
Dreaming of a Morgan Horse

JEANNE MELLIN

Ellen F. Feld

Blackjack is the herd boss at Willow Bend Morgans. He loves to be the center of attention and will push the other horses out of the way to get closer to any human visitor. Blackjack is a big showoff who likes to prance and stomp his feet, but when he hears the crinkle of a bag of carrots, he'll happily take a bow in the hopes a treat will come his way.

Breyer Animal Creations model of Blackjack,
sold with a copy of his book.

Ah, there's nothing like rolling in the mud!

Bob Moseder

Debbie ©'96

Frosty

Silvershoe Sunfrost
(Silvershoe Sundust x Miss Frosty Shadow)

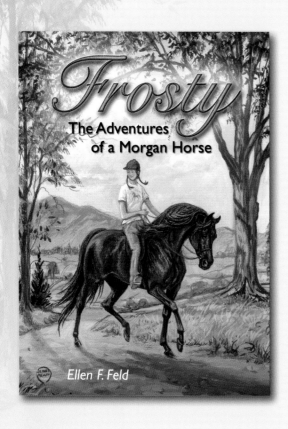

Frosty is a very rare gray Morgan. She has had five babies, all girls, and two of those are gray. Hopefully, there will be many more gray Morgan foals in Frosty's future. She is an incredibly sweet mare who loves to go trail riding and has a super-quick trot that is just as fast as many other horses' canters.

Rusty

Don Lee Rusty
(HM Royal Don x Soliloque Lisa)

All American Futurity III

New England Morgan Regional Horse

Bob Moseder

Rusty

The High-Flying Morgan Horse

Ellen F. Feld

Rusty is the ultimate versatile Morgan. He rides saddle seat, hunt seat, and western; jumps; drives; pulls a sleigh; and has even competed in barrel racing. His favorite pastime is trail riding, and if he crosses a stream or river, he always insists on stopping in the water and splashing with his front legs until his rider is drenched.

Bob Moseder

Robin

Soliloque Robin
(Soliloque Ian x Towne-Ayr Thistle)

Robin, like many of her pasture buddies, loves to be ridden fast! Her favorite gait is the trot, and she will happily trot for a long time, ears forward, eager to continue. If there's a brook, log, or other obstacle in her way, it's no problem. She'll look, sniff, and keep right on going.

Robin (foreground) and her friend Attie winning the Pairs class
at the New England Morgan Horse Show.

Annie

**Willow Bend Fiesta
(Double Black Knockout x
Silvershoe Sunfrost)**

Annie is one of
Frosty's daughters, but
unlike Frosty, Annie is
chestnut, not gray. Annie
is a big talker and will
whinny whenever she sees
people on the property,
no matter how far away
they are. If you talk back
to her, you can have a
long conversation because
she will respond to every
comment you shout at her
from afar.

Annie following her best friend
Rimfire wherever he goes.

Annie
The Mysterious Morgan Horse

Ellen F. Feld

Rimfire

CBMF No Exceptions
(GLB Bell Pepper x CBMF Winning Touch)

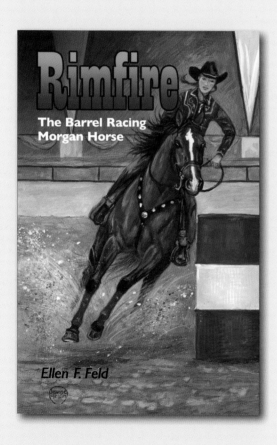

Rimfire with his best friend Annie.

Rimfire came to us after young Nicholas Feld won the Morgan in a national essay contest! Rimfire was just a baby when he arrived and Nicholas did all the early training himself. Originally trained western, Rimfire decided he wanted to be a saddle seat show horse. He had a great show career and now spends his time playing in the pasture with his best friend, Annie, and keeping an eye out for his boy, Nicholas.

Bob Moseder
© 2010

Sidekicks

Rerun

Willow

Shadow

Willow and Champ

Spot

Spot

Rerun

Future Stars

Luna, Lilly, Bandit

Luna

Bandit

Ginger

Diva